Dear Parent:
Your child's love of reading starts here!

Every child learns to read in a different way and at his or her own speed. You can help your young reader improve and become more confident by encouraging his or her own interests and abilities. You can also guide your child's spiritual development by reading stories with biblical values and Bible stories, like I Can Read! books published by Zonderkidz. From books your child reads with you to the first books he or she reads alone, there are I Can Read! books for every stage of reading:

SHARED READING
Basic language, word repetition, and whimsical illustrations, ideal for sharing with your emergent reader.

BEGINNING READING
Short sentences, familiar words, and simple concepts for children eager to read on their own.

READING WITH HELP
Engaging stories, longer sentences, and language play for developing readers.

READING ALONE
Complex plots, challenging vocabulary, and high-interest topics for the independent reader.

ADVANCED READING
Short paragraphs, chapters, and exciting themes for the perfect bridge to chapter books.

I Can Read! books have introduced children to the joy of reading since 1957. Featuring award-winning authors and illustrators and a fabulous cast of beloved characters, I Can Read! books set the standard for beginning readers.

A lifetime of discovery begins with the magical words **"I Can Read!"**

Visit www.icanread.com for information on enriching your child's reading experience.
Visit www.zonderkidz.com for more Zonderkidz I Can Read! titles.

"The LORD doesn't rescue by using a sword or a spear. And everyone who is here will know it. The battle belongs to the LORD."

—1 Samuel 17:47

ZONDERKIDZ

The Beginner's Bible David and the Giant
Copyright © 2008 by Zondervan
Illustrations © 2019 by Zondervan

Requests for information should be addressed to:
Zonderkidz, 3900 Sparks Drive SE, Grand Rapids, Michigan 49546

ISBN 978-0-310-76048-1

Illustrator: Denis Alonso

Printed in China

18 19 20 21 22 23 24 25 /DSC/ 15 14 13 12 11 10 9 8 7 6 5 4 3 2 1

David and the Giant

Goliath was a big giant.

He was mean.

He wanted to fight

King Saul's army.

The army was afraid.

They ran away from Goliath.

"We do not want to
fight you!" they cried.

David took care of sheep.

He loved God.

David's brothers were in
the king's army.

One day, David took food
to his brothers.
He heard about the giant.

David said, "The giant
does not scare me!"

"Let me fight the giant,"
David said to the king.
"God will help me."

"The giant is big,"
King Saul said.
"And you are too young."

"Please, let me fight him,"
said David.

So the king gave David
armor to wear.

David said,

"I do not need armor."

He was not used to wearing it.

David picked up some stones.

He was getting ready

to fight the giant.

David saw the giant.

The giant saw David.

"You are too small.

I will beat you!" said Goliath.

"You will not beat me,"
said David.

"God will help me!"

David took a stone.

He threw it at Goliath.

The stone hit Goliath
on the head.

Goliath fell down.

David won!

The men in Goliath's army
were scared.

They ran away.

The men in King Saul's army
were happy.

David was a hero.

"God is great!" yelled David.

"He helped me!"